Sharks

Kate Riggs

CREATIVE EDUCATION

seedlings

Published by Creative Education
P.O. Box 227, Mankato, Minnesota 56002
Creative Education is an imprint of
The Creative Company
www.thecreativecompany.us

Design by Ellen Huber
Production by Chelsey Luther
Art direction by Rita Marshall
Printed in the United States of America

Photographs by 123rf (cbpix), Alamy (Stephen Frink
Collection), Dreamstime (Vladislav Gajic), Getty Images
(Todd Bretl Photography), iStockphoto (Chris Dascher),
Shutterstock (Rich Carey, cbpix, Fotokon, KKulikov, fluke
samed, stockpix4u, Dray van Beeck), SuperStock (Mike
Agliolo, Minden Pictures, Norbert Wu)

Library of Congress Cataloging-in-Publication Data
Riggs, Kate.
Sharks / Kate Riggs.
p. cm. — (Seedlings)
Includes index.
Summary: A kindergarten-level introduction to sharks,
covering their growth process, behaviors, the oceans they
call home, and such defining physical features as their teeth.
ISBN 978-1-60818-342-5
1. Sharks—Juvenile literature. I. Title.

QL638.9.R55 2013
597.3—dc23   2012023777

First Edition
9 8 7 6 5 4 3 2 1

TABLE OF CONTENTS

Hello, Sharks! 4

Life in the Ocean 6

Toothy Fish 8

Fins and Rough Skin 10

Time to Eat! 13

Baby Sharks 14

What Do Sharks Do? 16

Goodbye, Sharks! 18

Picture a Shark 20

Words to Know 22

Read More 23

Websites 23

Index 24

Hello, sharks!

Sharks are big fish.

They live in
the oceans.

Sharks
have sharp,
pointy teeth.
They have
strong jaws.

Sharks have fins and a tail.

A shark's
skin is rough.
It feels like
sandpaper.

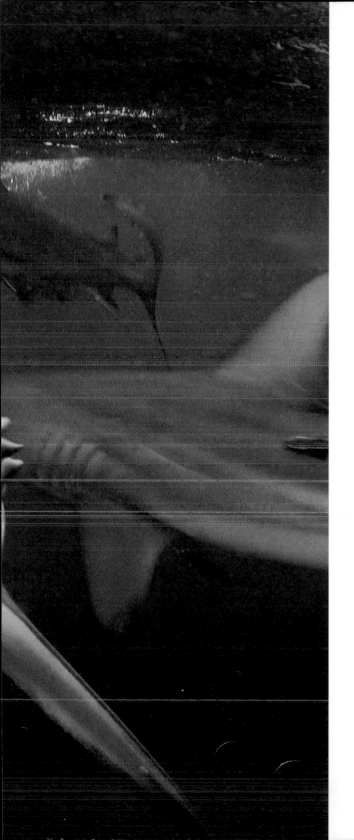

Most sharks eat meat. They eat fish and other ocean animals.

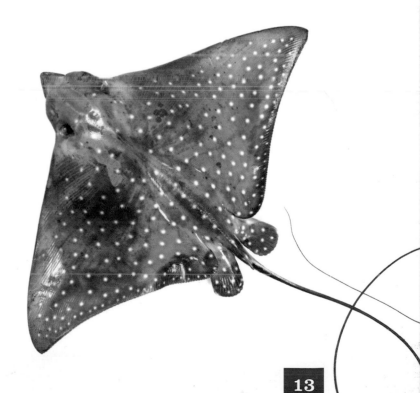

A baby shark
is called a
pup. A pup
usually grows
up by itself.

But some sharks live together in schools.

Sharks swim through the ocean.

They look for food.

Goodbye,
sharks!

Picture a Shark

gills

eye

snout

mouth

nostril

teeth

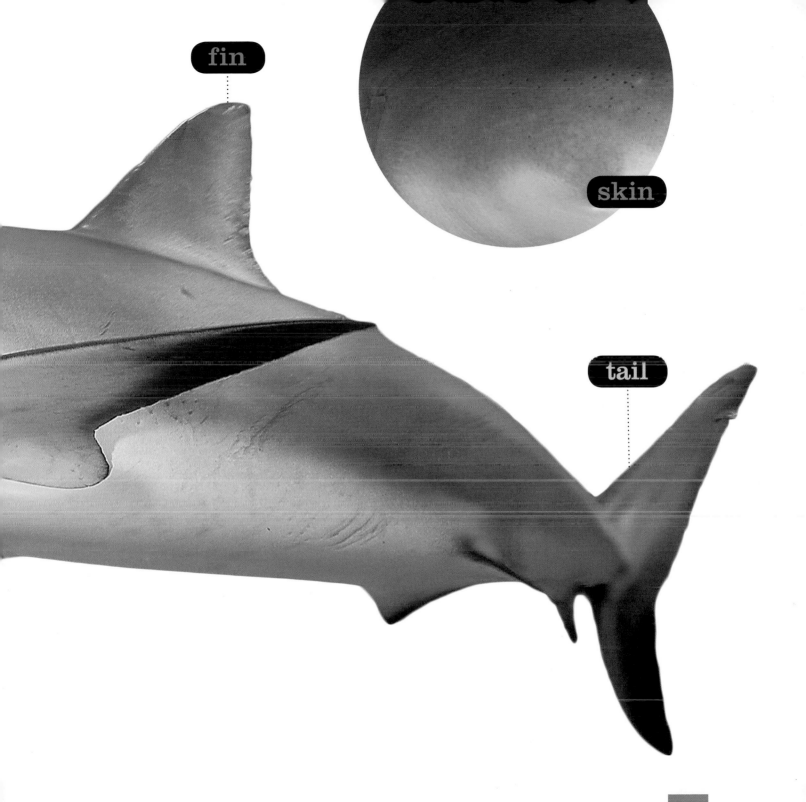

fin

skin

tail

21

Words to Know

fins: parts of a fish's body used for swimming

jaws: the upper and lower parts of the mouth

oceans: big areas of deep, salty water

schools: groups of fish, like sharks

Read More

Clarke, Ginjer. *Sharks!*
New York: Grosset & Dunlap, 2001.

Simon, Seymour. *Incredible Sharks*.
San Francisco: Chronicle Books, 2004.

Websites

Shark Activities
http://www.kidzone.ws/sharks/activities/index.html
Print out shark games or sheets to color. Put together
a puzzle online!

Sharks in the Classroom
http://www.enchantedlearning.com/subjects/sharks/
classroom/Classroomweblinks.shtm
Keep learning about sharks, with the help of fun activities.

Index

fins **10**
food **13, 17**
jaws **8**
oceans **7, 16**
pups **14**
schools **15**
skin **11**
swimming **16**
tails **10**
teeth **8**